EYE-BABY

Lawrence Sail was born in London in 1942 and brought up in the west country. A freelance writer, he has published eight collections of poems, most recently *Out of Land: New & Selected Poems* (1992), *Building into Air* (1995), *The World Returning* (2002) and *Eye-Baby* (2006), all from Bloodaxe Books. His poems have been broadcast on radio and television, and he also written a radio play. He has compiled and edited several anthologies, including *First and Always: Poems for Great Ormond Street Children's Hospital* (Faber & Faber, 1988), and (both with Kevin Crossley-Holland) *The New Exeter Book of Riddles* (Enitharmon Press, 1999) and *Light Unlocked: Christmas Card Poems* (Enitharmon Press, 2005). His *Cross-currents: Essays* (Enitharmon Press, 2005) contains forty-two essays written for *PN Review* and published in the magazine from 1995 to 2003.

He was editor of *South West Review* from 1981 to 1985, chairman of the Arvon Foundation from 1990 to 1994, director of the Cheltenham Festival of Literature in 1991 and co-director in 1999. He was awarded a Hawthornden Fellowship in 1992 and an Arts Council writer's bursary the following year. In 1991 he was a Whitbread Book of the Year judge; from 1994 to 1996 he was on the jury of the European Literature Prize. He has frequently worked abroad for the British Council, including visits to India, Egypt, Bosnia and Ukraine. He is a fellow of the Royal Society of Literature, and in 2004 he received a Cholmondeley Award from the Society of Authors.

LAWRENCE SAIL

EYE-BABY

BLOODAXE BOOKS

ISBN: 1 85224 729 0

First published 2006 by
Bloodaxe Books Ltd,
Highgreen,
Tarset,
Northumberland NE48 1RP.

www.bloodaxebooks.com
For further information about Bloodaxe titles
please visit our website or write to
the above address for a catalogue.

Bloodaxe Books Ltd acknowledges
the financial assistance of
Arts Council England, North East.

Cover printing by J. Thomson Colour Printers Ltd, Glasgow.

Printed in Great Britain by
Bell & Bain Limited, Glasgow.

For Grace and Rose

ACKNOWLEDGEMENTS

Acknowledgements are due to the editors of the following publications in which some of these poems first appeared: *Exeter Flying Post, Oxford Magazine, PN Review, Poetry Review, Quadrant* and *The Rialto*. 'A Travellers' Tale' was first published in *The Way You Say the World: A Celebration for Anne Stevenson* (Shoestring Press, 2003), 'Sparrowgrass' in *Poetry on a Plate: A feast of poems and recipes* (Salt Publishing, 2004), 'The Glimmering' in *Light Unlocked: Christmas Card Poems* and 'A Response to Rothko' in *Cross-currents: Essays* (both Enitharmon Press, 2005).

'Three Exeter Poems' was commissioned by the Northcott Theatre, Exeter; 'Light-shifts' by South Dartmoor Community College; and 'As a Bird' by BBC Radio 4 for National Poetry Day.

CONTENTS

Swimming in Italy

The pool shivers with lights,
a blue jelly refusing
to set, which organises
its own tides. Even in the dark
it harbours a second moon
to show up shameless dippers.

At one side, the pale shoots
of lavender suck in grey bees:
at the other, the oleander
dreams of hot ruins.
Overhead, a sky rinsed
daily to a new blankness.

And there, as vaguely elsewhere
as the feathery branches of the olive
which wave away on the breeze,
plough the swimmers, losing the world
even as they add it up,
counting it out in lengths.

Bosnia, 1996

This is the fridge. It lives in the garden
with its door open, alongside the gaping
jaw of the car plundered for parts.
Both are close to the burnt vines.

This, you can tell, is a private house.
You know by the scorch marks above the window frames,
the blackened roof-beams, the way that explosions
have skewed the whole thing on its broken foundations.

This is the bridge. On either side
it dips into the river as if,
trying to open the wrong way up,
it had fallen into its own reflection.

This is the night, where a black dog
lies curled awake, lacking the heart
to bark or sleep. There is unpicked fruit
on a tree whose name not many know.

These are American believers, going
To Medugorje. They are full of joy.
Each one is wearing a badge printed
with the words *Mary's Faithful Pilgrim*.

These marks on the ground are known today
As Sarajevo roses. They are what is left
when mortars are fired into a queue
of people waiting to buy bread.

These loud shouts are coming from people
driven to madness by the war, by grief.
Unlike those who have stepped on land mines,
they still have legs and run through the streets.

Visiting Akhmatova's Flat, Saint Petersburg

Six sparse rooms: their white-tiled stoves,
some memorabilia. Outside,
the canal dark, even under snow.

You always knew what not to lay claim to –
from glib prepositions to the grand temptations
which history sometimes offers a poet.

Not forty days, but thirty years –
and no solution, only a deepening
of the mystery: DEUS CONSERVAT OMNIA.

The known truth, waiting to be smuggled
through, despite all failings. Mandelstam's
blessing on you, yours on Brodsky.

In the Summer Gardens, the statues are already
sloughing off the grey wooden crates
in which they withstood the worst of winter.

The Glimmering

The horizon draws the line
at having been tamped down
all through a slutchy autumn,
moves in as a caul
of rain which blears the hills,
hissing like the prefix which history
adds to words and laughter:
finally, shrinks to the glimmering
from under a stable door,
a straw-breadth of light which can only
imply the warmth of spring
or the memory of it – the long
pursed buds of the lily
peeling open on the angel's wand.

Open Question

And what else
does the eye-mirror show
to the eye watching,
besides the head shorn
to the bone,
what else beyond
the pupillage
of its own closing ?

Scale

The pod of a boat
seed or kernel
braves the dark water,
riding the limitless flux,
insisting on the small-scale –
water scooped up
in a cupped hand:
a measure.

Child Holding a Yacht

The camera must be lying – he knew
as soon as he saw the picture, with the yacht
shrunk to fit snugly under his arm,
even with the sails hoisted and the burgee
run up at the masthead.

It told him nothing of the boat he manned –
how it fronted the waves, heeled smartly over
in a stiffening breeze, or gybed to change course,
or nodded at anchor, its hull ribbed
with the lagoon's clear light.

You'd never think, to look, that capes
had been rounded, enormous seas weathered,
the tanglements of the Sargasso outdone –
and he as navigator, crew, skipper,
single-handed in all this.

But when he saw in his own face the joy
which had him shouting wordlessly
and not quite knowing what to do –
in this at least, he had to admit,
the camera did not lie.

The Nightmare

Each time, the same:
his father standing
in the bedroom doorway,
staring in

But the truth was worse:
his father lost
in the gaining overfalls
of sea-change madness

Once he had radioed
the false bearings
there was no going back:
the trap worked itself

One lie broke
onto another:
the swell of them heaved,
racing to the horizon

Until deception
became delusion:
*I catch things almost
before they start falling*

Once he recalled
a photo: of himself
at seven, proudly
holding a yacht

And more than once
he saw himself standing
in a doorway, returning
his son's stare

Notes for the Ship's Log

(for Peter Scupham)

1

Such is the course steered across
the cunning theatre of the sea, with its deft
transformations, from first word to last,
indefinite to imperative.

2

Cargo of common dust, quintessence
of all that rises and falls: the manifest
drawn up to allow for any number
of possible shapes and guises.

3

Un peu d'histoire for sure, the memory's
box-room of toys: and assorted structures
from hutments to outrageous palaces
of purest sugar-candy.

4

Passage made through the nightmare tropics,
the lush green fields of calenture
laid wavily out as far as the horizon,
tempting to lie down in.

5

Hallucinations brought on, perhaps,
by rancid lobscouse: and, persisting,
the realisation that we are headed
beyond the projected world.

6

As ultimate promotion of dust, the presence
of ghosts gathered, at dusk, in the rooms
of the dying. Their endless patience. The weight
of their commanding absences.

7

Many, by now, the figures on deck,
their faces upturned, as if questing:
as if they knew that Ararat must be
a landfall of saving words.

Receding

The ferry bears away –
watching England disappear
astern is not simple, not
a matter of there
one moment, gone the next.

At first the grey cliffs
hardly shrink, and even
after the harbour wall
has lost its outlines
its lights go on pinpointing themselves.

Nothing dramatic – a withdrawal
so stealthy, so inch by inch
that you cannot be quite sure
of the moment at which
the land is no longer there.

Only a slow bleaching
into blankness, sadder than it really is –
and all the way over, drowning
the pulse of the engines,
the ship's foghorn, lowing.

Stowaways

Blind passengers, reduced
to pure anxiety, their spirits
rise and fall with each lift
and plunge of the butting hull:
bracing themselves, they test
the strength of their old visions.

Some, discovered after food
has gone missing from the galley,
or given away by a whiff
of tobacco seeping through a bulkhead,
are simply tipped overboard
as if they were so much trash.

Others, airborne, are undone
by cold – cold which unpicks,
finger by numbed finger,
their hold on a strut, slides them,
helpless, out from the wheelbay
into a shroud of thin air.

Falling through cloud or water,
perhaps their last recall
is the iron taste of blood,
the danger of not leaving,
or the far horizon bright
and burnished as New Jerusalem.

What is certain becomes so
only late on, when the stowaways
re-emerge, insistent phantoms,
at the point where memory rounds
on experience, and well within sight
of the dark relief of land.

Parenthetic

The brim of high water
and the sea turned
in on itself,
swaying, moiré,
settled for once
in the broad arms of the bay.

(The shoreline hardly
fringed with salt,
transparent as a river,
and pebbles shifted
with a softness closer
to sand than to knuckled stone.)

Overhead, samples
of arranged skies –
on the left, red
over yellow, slipping
from a shelf of front,
on the right, a rebirth of blue.

(Dead centre, a roil
of purple storm-cloud
with gulls rousant,
and a shaft of light
beamed down as if
in search of a saintly focus.)

Without attribution
the ocean authorises
each version of itself
simply, by change
and chance, outflanking
any graft of feeling.

(And is no more aligned
to the soulful beach-walkers
than to the helmsmen
of those two yachts
in the middle distance
riding their luck from A to B.)

Altdorfer's *Saint George and the Dragon*

The dying beast
has become absurd,
a deflated puffball,
its energy collapsed to
a cartoon of dismay

It has nothing to compare
with the swelling rump
of the white charger,
its impatient hooves
and proud head

Or the darkly glinting
armour of the knight
slumped in the saddle,
exhausted or at ease,
his lance lowered

The knight, around whom
the Hercynian forest
deploys its huge splays,
its world-wall which will reach
from earth to sky

A Response to Rothko

A picture lives by companionship,
expanding and quickening in the eyes
of the sensitive observer. It dies
by the same token.

Transgressions of the frame: the subject leaning
its elbow out of the canvas. The cloak's
crimson lining that spills,
molten, onto wood.

And *vice versa*, the nightmare world
sucked in, banged up in a box, glazed:
here, the worst of horror
is drained of blood.

By the same token, the citizens of art's
republic of loneliness struggle towards
hope, a horizon beyond
the surrounding truths.

King and Queen
(for Ivan and Lissa Campbell)

This is the story: as the sculptor played with a bit
of modelling wax, it became a head with horns
and a beard. As soon as the horns turned to a crown
he recognised the head of a king, who would need
a queen, to be complete.

For fifty years they have sat on their bench of stone,
looking out from the shelter of each other. Knowledge
is a slight curvature of the spine; patience, the sky
and its lights caught in the single eye each has,
passing endlessly on.

South is their kingdom, where moonlight cannot reach
the blurred suburbs of sunken cities; where clouds
languish over African forests, and wolves are so rare
they must be a wavy mirage born of the intense
white-out of noonday heat.

South where you two, as your photos show, masquerade
as regal alter egos, figures languidly reclining
on Moroccan sand: one stylishly stretched out,
the other sitting at ease, calm and smiling
into the uncertain haze.

As if you already sensed that an expedition
begun with love, with luck would find the way
which leads from double vision to a singular view,
from desert to desire, mirage to marriage – a story
less of discovery than recognition.

In the Auction House

Somewhere between the idea
and the dry tap of the hammer,
in the long traverse from author
to auction, from pen to paddle,
time and chance have rendered
whole lives to lots.

In this there is less of Larkin
with his England *going*, *going*,
soon gone – and more, perhaps,
of Thor's hammer as it swings
in Heaney's *North*, between
geography and trade.

Enter, too, the auctioneer
from *Moortown*, described by Hughes –
a man with cattle to sell
to reluctant bidders who know
history and the distance between
worth and price.

But even those Devon farmers
might be frankly amazed
at what can be penned, as here,
together under one roof –
on this floor, for instance, a currency
entirely of paper:

while upstairs, seated at the virginals,
is a young woman whose price
must surely outfly all guesswork –
her yellow shawl ballooning
as if suddenly caught up
by a feverish squall.

Surrealist Negatives

No engine advances on air from the boarded fireplace,
the flames are out on the fine neck of the giraffe,
the seven drawers ascending the woman are shut.
On the stairs, all the figures but one have completed
their descent successfully. No telephone is caught
in the lobster pots. No black flags are billowing
on the shore of the dream. No unblinking eye
wags from side to side on the metronome.
Donkeys are safe, the forests and cities re-peopled.
The urinal is once again connected to the plumbing.
The glass of water is just what it says it is.
Everything has been invented, nothing discovered.

A Matter of Focus

Yes, they can see the chair —
high-backed, unyielding, set
at an angle by the large window.
But they see also that for sure
nothing is waiting to happen.
Which is why, perhaps, no one enters,
though the single door is ajar:
not a skipping child, not a cat,
not a woman reading a letter
and certainly not an old man
with unkempt hair, sallow skin,
and dressed entirely in black,
including his ink-shiny waistcoat
crossed by a gold watch-chain.
No one will ever see
the way in which his thin lips
chew at themselves, sourly,
with rhythm of a kind. And even
beyond the window there is nothing
but a pall of slack air.
If you like, though, there do exist
more details about the chair.

La Mouche de Holub

Dans le langage corporel de leur propre profession
les objets peuvent garder leur unique image
de pot, arbre, marée empiétant –
et même les ailes de la mouche de Holub,
au lustre vert-de-noir, peuvent rester intactes
en passant par *fly, Fliege, sinek, mosca*,
tous les Babel des désignations humaines.

Mais faire que le son et le rythme précis
du vol franchissent sans dommage les frontières
de l'air, accompagnés des silences qu'invoque
chaque mot placé par la langue – parvenir
à convertir en présent le passé que recèle
toute traduction: c'est ça qui assure
que le cerveau du traducteur ne cesse jamais de vrombir.

Holub's Fly

In the body language of their stated selves
objects may keep their singular image
as pot, tree, the inroading tide –
and even the wings of Holub's fly,
with their green-black gloss, be held intact
through *mouche, Fliege, sinek, mosca*,
all the Babels of human naming.

But to have the exact sound and rhythm
of its flight borne safely over the frontiers
of air, along with the silences invoked
by each word tongued – somehow, to make
of the past concealed in all translation
a present tense: it's that which keeps
the translator's mind endlessly buzzing.

Eyeballing

You bet that *I is another*!
But who can really tell whether
this another is really other
or that man or woman, rather,
always to be found regathered
in the dwarf reflection tethered
in the eye of a friend like a brother,
who himself is reflected further
in the eye of the opposite other?
Image of self-conceit fractured
by a dominant fear of Lethe –
clownish midget messiah
who self-repeats over and over
One thinks me, so I have fans.

Sonnet des Prunelles

Je est un autre – ah, oui!
Mais qui est-ce qui sait vraiment si
cet autre est vraiment autrui
ou plutôt celle ou celui
qui est toujours reproduit
dans le reflet nain pris
dans l'œil d'un vrai ami
qui se reflète, lui aussi,
dans l'œil en face de lui?
Image de la suffisance qui,
craignant surtout l'oubli,
fait le pitre, petit messie
qui sans arrêt se redit
On me pense, donc on me suit.

Sparrowgrass

(for Helen)

Butter-wet, lickerous,
tender tongue-tie,
wilt-headed fasces,
maytime mouth-melt,
work of the fingers,
lips and tongue,
more a bird
in hand than in the bush –
and offering a way
to recover a baby's
unashamed delight,
afterwards, by sucking
each finger clean.

White Peach

Under the skin,
itself rose soft
but tough, bitter,
the flesh, firm
yet tender
to the knife,
dense with sugars

The flesh, white
not yellow,
white at the border
of green, the colour
of iceberg roses,
with the pallor of illness
at its most alluring

Long before
you reach the stone-heart
with its hard ridges,
you will be up
to your elbows
in runnels of juice,
your fingers dripping

And memory, turned
informer, will tell
that you know already
this bitter-sweetness
you fear and desire –
the linger of it
on your drenched lips

Three Exeter Poems

The House that Moved

The streetlight peers onto ghosts, ruins,
history driving a coach and horses
through any settlement – and here
is a house that has grown its own legs,
has shaken itself and is ready to move,
cheered on by the citizens.

The faces of clocks can only display
their set expressions and round figures –
but here is the evidence never quite caught
in the stare of the camera's soulless eye:
the city's towers will be rebuilt,
and the house move.

Repairing the Clock Tower

Taking the clock apart – the face
without the hands, the hands walking
away as legs, leaving the racehorses
to plunge on with no post to pass:
leaving echoes of the bass, the throaty sax,
the last drumbeat.

While the dapper band quicksteps time away,
the busker masquerading as sole survivor
works the crowd with his squeezebox, his songs
out of season. Enter the future
showing only as snow on the banks of screens:
a dream city.

Evidence

Doing time, the prisoner on the roof
holds red smoke sky-high, as a pound sign,
or the mirror image of Britain. He shares
the air with the gold-fire pennons on the towers
of the great cathedral anchored in its green,
harbouring the word.

Two among many faceted images
which cluster in the fly's eye, in a room
immune to doubt and the new graffiti
on the wall, the hopes and fears of all
us little brothers and sisters, who are covered
from every angle.

City Limits

Street lamps, cameras leaning down,
witnesses in waiting, steady
as blue lights never are.

Inscribed portals, ageing statues,
Latin recycled on walls
as tags or anagrams of rage.

Locked parks, boarded-up houses,
never enough to absorb
the echo of riches hoarded.

Rules of engagement: one, never ask
the young where their money comes from,
or the old, where theirs has gone.

On Swagger Street the old don't show up:
for teenagers, Temperance Drive
is way beyond no-go.

Only at night does the verve of the city
break through to joy flayed
to the raw meat of its nerves.

From Petra

1

Whole cliff-faces worn
wondrously by the hot wind
to mottled rashers of stone

Yet across the thresholds
nothing but silence, less
soft than the rock, echoless

Space meagrely scooped,
a baffle of darkness, culs-dc-sac,
not even the way to Avernus

A darkness from which to turn
back to the shrinking shadows
of noonday, the beating light

Even, to suffer in silence
the long persistence of the flies
raging all round your head

2

There is something between
the rockface and the eye
some interference
a veil of white threads
or finely scratched glass

What is observed
is far from solid,
far from impossible,
a city engulfed,
cire perdue

Or a seal worn down
unevenly, pressed
into the wax
of the molten rock
and, slightly, blurring

Still readable
are porticoes, pediments,
involuted
crenellations,
emerging or fading

It glows less
rose-red than pink,
the colour you might
imagine for the inside
walls of a dream

Fountains

Part of the culture,
you could say, with a backdrop
of lavish palaces,
triumphalist boulevards,
extravagant gardens.
And apt for disguises –
shaving-brush bristles
of foam, plumes,
sly squirts
from the mouths of dolphins
or the necks of urns,
or arcing back
in a little boy's
stream of piss.

Water that splatters
back to the surface,
plentiful, ready
to resume itself,
to be used as a template
for shape, again
and again, like words –
the way that a poem
by Apollinaire
might flower on the page
as a spray or fountain.

But already the basin
is drying out,
the pipework starting
to choke. Soon
there will be little
but the crackle of leaves
brittle as pappadums,
scraping on stone.

Sensed

1

At the turn of the path
where the earth becomes dusty...

Where is the thinking ghost,
the shadow self?

Each chime of the clock
a dent hammered into
the smooth surface of dreaming

And the thick fragrance
of night-flowers flooding the garden...

Who is lying, heart racing,
in the room with drawn curtains?

At the turn of the path
where the trees close in
all your possible dreams are hidden

2

The wind falters in the leaves
a voice trailing
into forgetfulness

Hanks of rain drive
over the dark
lure of the lake

Hardly to be glimpsed, a hand
draws heavy
curtains closer

In the leaves, the wind begins
to stir again, squaring
up to the night

In a Dream
(for Elizabeth)

Two people on a West Yorkshire hillside,
sitting side by side on a wall, dangling
their legs over the edge, like kids.
Someone says, very softly, *I love you.*
Someone else leans a head on a shoulder.
They look straight ahead, at the chestnut trees
Hanging their splays over dusty ground.

And someone knows that, just out of sight
below the wall, even this far inland,
seethes an ocean of storms which will never
subside: and is at a loss how to tell
the innocent other, or even how
to wake to the possible consequence
of putting such happiness at risk.

Catechism

What are you looking at?
The baffle in your eye.

What do you see?
The depths of the real.

How are you justified?
Hardly, if at all.

Where are your parents?
Buried apart.

Where is your wife?
In forgotten dreams.

Where are your children?
Escaped to their lives.

Of whom do you dream now?
Too many to name.

What do you give?
Too little, too much.

What do you take?
Too much, not enough.

How long have you got?
Too little for redress.

What things make you glad?
Too many to count.

What makes you ashamed?
Inaction, excuses.

What makes you lament?
The world's madnesses.

What makes you hopeful?
Those who try.

Anything else?
The love in your eye.

In the Bar Italia
(for Erica)

You could say, with reason, that almost
nothing is happening beyond
the flicking of the overhead fan,
its languorous division of the air
into blades of shadow and light.

The beige formica refuses
either to absorb or reflect,
the slowly revolving spiral
of coffee lies perfectly wound
into the bubbled froth.

In her momentary absence
it comes upon him, a force
of feeling enough, almost,
to jump him sideways for joy.

Sentence

Beware of that hiss, that little platform
like the BBC tape labelled *Outside Atmosphere*,
which you hear nowadays before you speak,
though it never used to be there – as though
one part of ageing could be to apprehend
everything you say as a pre-recording
in which speech stiffens to vatic utterance.

Alalia

The moment before the dodgem car
slews to a halt,
when pumping the pedal
does nothing: all power gone.

Some of the dying do not
speak when they reach
this point of truth;
as if they had seen through something.

Neither do they invite
queries. The people
who are in the room
will simply go on waiting.

As the room alters around them:
as the ghosts also
wait. As the room
softly becomes an anteroom.

And here, swinging from car
to car, comes the man
with the wide grin
to collect everybody's money.

At the Bedside

Perhaps it is not, after all,
the whole story which races
through the heads of the dying, with the gloss
of last words in waiting –
but some inconsequential detail
which just happens to have stuck.

Say, for instance, the taste
of a boiled egg eaten, when a child,
in St Austell, by a window looking
out over kaolin mountains.
The sweetness of the yolk against
the tangy bread and butter.

Or the perfect round of apples
at the foot of a tree in Brittany
so scrawny as to make fruit seem
miraculous. It looked as if
it had shed them all at once
as a single golden earth-halo.

Or the view of the old bridge
at Mostar, its high brow
soaring and swooping above
the Neretva. Or the drugging smell
of red valerian, or the feel
of silk rubbed between the fingers.

But perhaps such images are only
the journeys of wishing and warding
for those who wait by the bed,
for whom also it is late,
and who cannot ignore the tut
and sigh of the morphine shunt.

The Edge: Remembering Romano

This year more than ever, it seems,
the house is festooned with swooping birdsong;
longer than ever the vines' twisting travels,
heavier their fruit in the weighing hand;
deeper the evening glow on the stubble,
keener the bladed light on the earth;
taller the spill of the olive tree, broader
the jigsaw of fig-leaves close to the pool.

And part of all this is the force of your smile,
your love of giving, the brimming armfuls
of melons or lettuce, your lively alliance
with everything natural, everything quick:
greater than ever the real value
of your gone presence giving fullness its edge.

A Holiday Snap

Thirty summers ago, on a dusty footpath
somewhere in the Dolomites, the air
heavy with heat and resin, he must have turned
round and thought what a good picture it would make –

his mother in her red cardigan, white blouse
and blue denim skirt, making her way gingerly
down a rough stairway of slate, dwarfed between
the surrounding forest's soaring pillars of fir trees.

Somehow the camera saw more than he bargained for –
when the prints came back, no gloss could disguise
how small she was, how vulnerable despite
the pluck and cheerfulness she'd always shown.

It was all here – the irritable duets,
his intolerance, her fine traps of tears,
the choking closeness of home, the old progression
of anger, guilt, anger at guilt: but now

for the first time, and long before her death,
he saw, in one sharp frame, how little he could help her
as she made her way through angled shade and sunlight,
the loose slate skittering on itself under her feet.

Classic

Not the dark but the silence
is the real dread,
not the impossibility
of evading the gleaming river
which swarms under the hull,
not even the triple failure
to bark of the dog's heads,
but the ferryman's absolute
refusal to speak
or acknowledge the dead.

Pen

Extruded between
a tripod of digits,
it is poised as the outermost
muscle of the mind
over the paper
in that instant before
it stoops to its shadow
to channel its flux
of black glister

And here already
come the adamant words
to whose making
the pen always points,
the little glyphs
which hardly dig
into the nap
surface impressions
streaming into light

Frisks of pattern
commute to the eye
then back to the mind,
black and gold
like the wind across water
in winter: and the pen
itself lances
the world, writing
its book of changes

From *And yet* to *As if*

And yet... at this precise moment
the brake goes on, the scale swings back
to even Stevens, at both ends
of the seesaw feet squirm in the air,
the *via media* staking its claim:
the fulcrum hefts a double weight,
the trimmer balances the rocking
boat, poets balance their books.

And precisely after this moment comes
the adrenaline rush, the craving for an outright
refusal, the urge to kick over tables,
lob glasses at the cowardly barman,
stomp outside to shout home truths
at the blue moon, before escaping
in a drunken boat headed for the last
isle of sweet excesses... *As if.*

Convalescing at the Coast

Nothing to equal
the width of the sands,
the lapping curves of the bay:
the foreshore streams
with smoke conjured
from every curling wave.

Each figure is
a reduced widow
against the light of day:
something has disarmed you
more than you know,
more than words can say.

Nothing quite fits –
not the man semaphoring
to the kite rippling like a plaice,
nor the family huddled
close to the dunes,
shivering under a sunshade.

Thanks to the stimulating
air, I even
wrote a few trifles, although
a good deal of sand
sifted onto
the paper. I felt really well…

Thus Thomas Mann
at eighty, recalling
his July beach-hut, in a letter
dated the tenth
of the eighth – two days
before his death inland.

Reprise

Your friends have taken to telling you
tales about yourself – for instance,
how once you led the way
at night into a closed
and dusty alpine hotel,
where you slept in the ghostly ballroom
and fell through the rotted joists.

Or how, one summer Sunday,
you were caught in the rain together
in a small skiff, and took shelter
under the arch of a bridge
where you ate a bagful of sweets
and anything might have happened.

And someone else has never
forgotten the words exchanged
apparently when you met him
coming out of the cinema
in Walton Street, on the day
that Kennedy was shot.

And even the voice of a stranger
reminds you that when he left
you told him to keep in touch,
which is why he is ringing now
in the hope of coming to see you
with the family – just a few nights.

This is simply what the past
can still do, the way it takes you
on to reprise or reprisal,
or re-invents you deftly
in the errors memory makes:
adjusting its facets, collecting
enough anecdotes for a wake.

Twin Babies Waking

Rose

Drumming the air
with all four limbs
rigid, goes with
the daily manifesto's
exultant shout.

Such force, given
the proper attachments,
could surely power
a moderate village, or
a one-woman orchestra.

Grace

The world is there
to be observed,
taken in, studied,
its textures tested
one by one.

The day begins
with a slight frown
indicating that work
on the great research project
has now resumed.

Feeding the Dolls

The two year olds
are feeding their dolls
air sandwiches
crammed with promises –
and brought at a run
from the bright kitchen
endlessly stocked
with imagination
and their delight.

The dolls are sitting
in bloated collapse,
stomachs out,
heads hanging –
as over-full
as the hog flung
down from the ramparts
of Carcassonne
to show the besiegers
that there really was
food to spare
in the suffering city.

Working Back

The future has arrived, a preview
in the form of two girl putti –
two, since you'd no more expect it
to be single, than think that a cyclops
would be much good at squinting.

They entertain each other
with possibilities, invent
new noises, improbable
hand gestures, take it in turns
to act the part of echo.

Lying back in the bath
after a hairwash, they look
as driftily composed as Ophelia,
their features ruffed in foam.
They do not understand death.

But still they like to align
alternatives, rehearse
the little mantra which explains:
Mummy out, Daddy here
or *Mummy here, Daddy gone.*

If one wakes in tears,
the other looking anxiously on,
it is not a matter of pain
but the shock of losing a dream.
They are working back to the present.

The Puzzle

And the word made bone was at first
the budding frame of a baby
in its baggy skin:
and dwelt among us, easily
outlasting its quilt of flesh.

In time it also became
evidence beyond contention –
fractured, stove in
or set out on shelves, an index
of bundled tibias and skulls.

Wobble-headed child
of Christmas, supine or propped
on blue, trying
to frown the world into focus,
for you this is yet to come:

the puzzle of how to read
the non-identical twins
of judgement and love,
how to count the broken bones
and still reach out for rejoicing.

From the Uncut Rushes

The first take proposes
everything in the room
as only a function of time,
unwashed sand – from
the high chairs side by side
to the two candles lopsidedly
melting, to the flat gray
of autumn light at the window.

Take two, however, has
survivors intent on themselves,
on each other's company, amid
the wood harbouring light,
the stubborn ramparts of wax,
the imagined I of eternity
twinned with the dry clock,
broken into real plurals.

Light-shifts
(for Heather Stimson)

What, before A, after Z, could begin
to whirl the water, or pierce the dark
and make the salt waves glint like sequins?

A breeze swoops through the fields, repeats
itself as a perfect curve, riffles
the bristling avenues of wheat.

Overhead, a bird displays its wingbones
X-rayed against the sun: at dusk,
fireflies fizz in the hedgerow.

And even at sea, the foam ignites
flickers of fire, where the lighthouse's beam
blares its all-round brightness.

It is part of the same idea that races
from the gushing clarinet, that flutters in the flute
or rattles on the drum's moonface.

It is there in the heavy flowerheads which track
the path of the sun, in the banging of the moth
which the fierce lamp draws back.

And even the early ghosts trapped
by the lens or the pen are on the move, slowly
fading from the paper's nap.

Here, after A, before Z, come the shine
and dance, the word and what it describes –
movement and light in unbroken lines.

Syringa

Cutesy, with that ra-ra frill
at the hem of each flower –
and you've clearly been using
eye make-up again, to give
that bruised and needy look.
And some, no doubt, would think well
of those anthers prinked with yellow.

It can't last, of course,
a few downpours
will be enough
to burn your soft skin brown.
But by then, forget flirtation –
one whiff of you, and the garden
is crammed with lost souls.

Blue Iris

You flower in tatters,
your yellow and blue
rainbow polarities
an ensign run up
from bladed leaves
after a struggle.

There is something unflower-like
about you, and dangerously
exposed, as the twist
of your tubers is exposed,
even something
unbecoming.

Your flame continues
to flicker from
its last redoubt
of washed blue.
That, also, is
imprinted on the eye.

A Travellers' Tale

After the dusty nightmare drive through the mountains
where roadside shrines leaned with their little doors
sagging open, and rusted cars were breaking
out of time on the plunging scree, they came
to Apollonia, where the dusklight had already retired
to its misty retreat on the lake.

Not speaking Greek, they wandered like vacant dreamers
past the warm coronas of candles glimpsed through the portal
of a church, then on through a few lit stalls displaying
honey, halva and fruit, drawn by a waft
of music to a ring of trees with whitewashed trunks
where some dancers were calmly swaying.

All of them wore black – and not one, you'd guess,
was under seventy: absorbed, knowing each step,
they moved with ease yet seemed a world away,
enclosed in their own rhythms... The travellers found
a place to eat, and ordered what they wanted
by pointing, since they could not say.

On the way back to their cheap hotel, they discovered
the dancers gone, and silence guarding their absence
with a version of power the still air could not define.
A few yards on, the church stood in darkness, folded
shut. That night they hardly slept, and rose early
to escape the mosquitoes' whining.

It was only when they got close to the border, with nothing
to declare, that they sensed just how far they had gone
out of their way, on a loop past age and youth
through a zone of forgiving ghosts where acceptance seemed
common as goosegrass, and love itself an eye-baby
dancing in the eye of truth.

A Note to the Inheritors

Whatever readings
glow from screens
or from the surety
of your new starts
believe them only half:

just as we
cannot quite know
how it felt
in the hardly paid
legions of a dying empire,

so you, searching
for what hooked down
Holocene man
should not quite trust
the easy apparent symbols,

whether of Venice
listing into
the swelling water
or the wild flowers shooting
head-high from ancient motorways:

and perhaps even
in your time the old
arrangements will persist –
un-newsworthy, complex,
any age's dark gold.

As a Bird

Whether or not you agree that it's fair to describe
the imagination as a bird, here it goes again
in its flight of fancy mode, lifting up and away
from the city streets – the food outlets, the stink
of pot pourri in gift shops, *Big Issue* sellers,
sharp-suited men briefed to market the truth,
bargain hunters, and the homeless, lying on the green.

The fine cathedral itself is swiftly reduced
to a stand-up model which must surely be held together
with tucked-in flanges and glue. The imagination
soon has the whole of Devon in its view –
the working sump of the moor, the delving combes,
the light-fissured rivers, the two coasts cushioned in foam,
the seamarks, the loom of lights beneath the horizon.

Even time, at this remove, is no more
a problem than space – in Teignmouth, for example,
sunk in a Mexican wave of wind-driven rain,
John Keats is still nursing poor Tom, while further north
Ted Hughes continues to take the elemental
brunt of underworlds, and track the spirits
which quicken Shakespeare, salmon, fox and flower.

And just across the border, three silhouettes
outlined against the great dish of the moon
in its summer fullness, are high on the rich air
of the Quantocks. Imagination chooses to place
Coleridge in the lead, garrulous, ecstatic –
with brother and sister Wordsworth doing their best
to keep up, while avoiding roots and rabbit-holes.

Sooner or later, though, there has to be
a coming down to earth, a confrontation
with the blank veto of paper or screen, the tug
of need and background noise. What you then must imagine
is coaxing that bird down from the air, still singing:
and a way somehow to take your true bearings,
to find in the word, even this late on, a beginning.

At the Turn

Nothing is set
at nought, or seems
to come of age:
in the garden, a pert
blackbird chips
at silence, a whiff
of camphor comes off
the smoke tree glowing
in its long late blush.

Its leaves flare
from green to acid
yellow, with veins
which stay red
and so fine
they could not be immune
to hurt. Then they turn
crimson, magenta,
blood-red, murrey.

Now, as they break
away, it is clear
how utter, uncountable
they are: how time
alone could not measure
each one
turning in its glory
as it drifts down
to the dark earth.